Englisch-Stars

3

Erarbeitet von

Barbara Gleich
Irene Reindl
Britta Schmid
Katrin Schmidt

Illustriert von

Martina Mair und
Wilfried Poll

Oldenbourg

Inhalt

Hello 3
Colours 5
Numbers 8
At school 11
Body and feelings 14
Toys 17
Clothes 20
Weather and days 23
Family and friends 26
Drinks 30
Breakfast 32
Fruit 35
Pets 38
Our nature 41
Farm animals 44
Great Britain 47
Picture dictionary 49

1. Fill in.

My ________

____

____

2. Number in the correct order.

3. What do they say? Write.

Good night.
Good afternoon.
Good evening.
Good morning.

1. Find the words and draw lines.

2. What's Sally's favourite colour? Do the crossword.

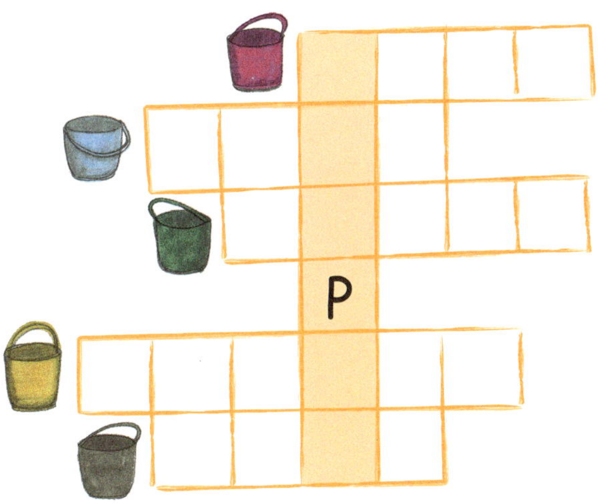

grey
yellow
blue
green
pink

Verbinde mit den richtigen Farben. Achtung, zu zwei Bildern gehören mehrere Farben.

3. Draw lines.

grey
blue
black
green
red
brown
yellow

4. Write and colour.

yellow
green
white
red
purple
grey

Was soll das denn heißen?

Da sind Buchstaben durcheinandergekommen. Schreibe erst das Wort, male dann den Pinsel in der richtigen Farbe an.

5. Find the words and circle them.

y	m	a	b	j	l	g
e	o	g	r	e	e	n
l	r	g	o	h	b	h
l	a	e	w	d	l	a
o	n	a	n	v	u	u
w	g	a	g	r	e	y
r	e	d	c	u	k	p
f	g	n	i	z	h	u
o	b	w	h	i	t	e

orange	**brown**
green	**yellow**
red	**white**
grey	**blue**

6. What colour is missing? Write.

red + **blue** = ______________

______________ + **blue** = **green**

yellow + ______________ = **orange**

black + **white** = ______________

1. Write the numbers in the correct order.

2. Count and write.

3. Do you know the word? Write.

nine → ______

five → ______

seven → ______

one → ______

eight → ______

ten → ______

4. How many lollies? Trace the lines and write.

 ______ lollies

 ______ lollies

 ______ lollies

 ______ lollies

5. How much is it? Write.

three + one = ____________

two + five = ____________

three + six = ____________

four + one = ____________

ten – seven = ____________

five – four = ____________

seven – five = ____________

nine – eight = ____________

6. Correct or wrong? Tick.

	correct	wrong
There are **two**  .	○	○
There is **one**  .	○	○
There are **eight**  .	○	○
There are **seven**  .	○	○

1. Number.

1 schoolbag
2 book
3 folder
4 ruler
5 pencil case
6 pencil
7 rubber
8 scissors
9 glue

2. Draw lines.

lollipop lady
board
teacher
chalk
desk
pen
picture
poster
computer

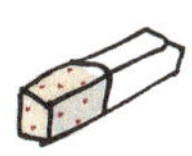

3. Odd one out.

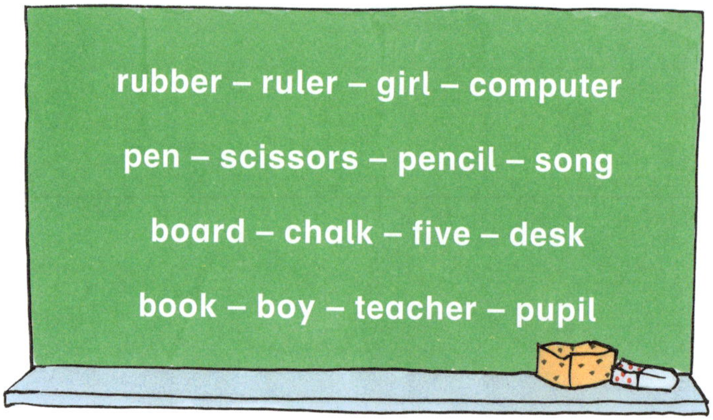

4. Read, look and write. What's missing?

What's missing on Steve's desk?

The ______________ is missing.

What's missing on Kathy's desk?

The ______________ is missing.

What's missing on Polly's desk?

The ______________ is missing.

5. Read and colour.

The pencil case is green.

The ruler is yellow.

The pen is red.

The pencil is blue.

The rubber is pink.

The lollipop is purple.

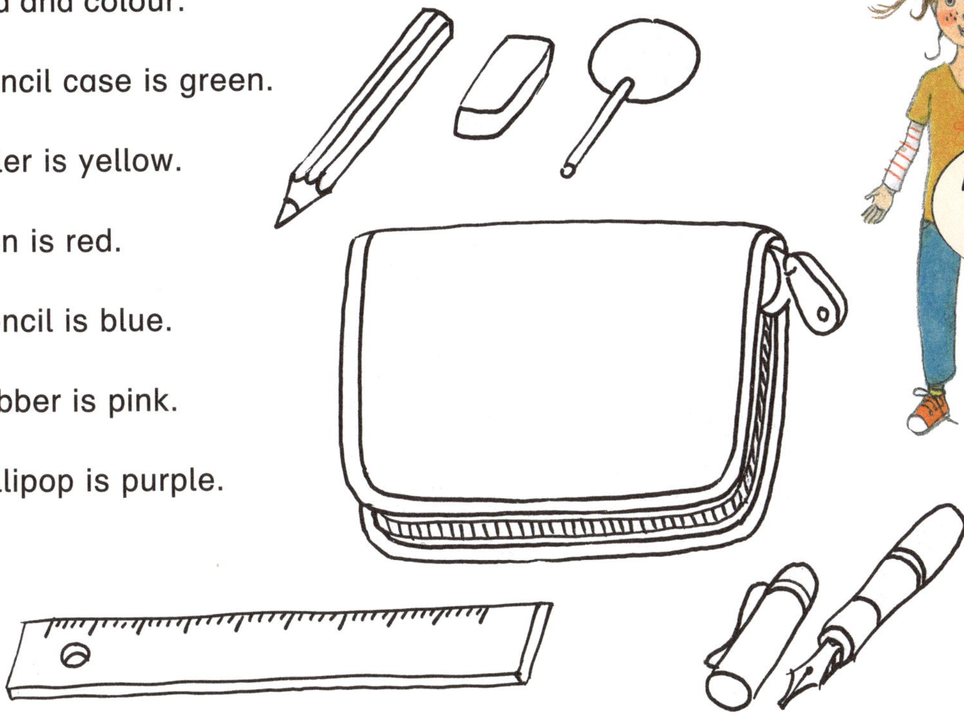

6. What belongs into the schoolbag? Write.

pencil **ruler**
scissors **pencil case**
desk **chalk** **board**
poster **folder**
pen **glue** **rubber**
computer **book**

Finde die Wörter senkrecht und waagrecht. Kreise sie ein. Trage sie dann unten richtig ein.

1. Find the words and circle them. Fill in.

n	b	o	d	y	t	u	r	z	l	u	q
s	h	a	n	d	s	x	c	b	e	l	v
f	a	w	a	r	m	s	p	y	g	m	h
e	s	q	r	b	m	l	o	p	s	y	a
e	c	v	e	f	o	o	t	a	b	u	i
t	h	y	b	t	j	k	h	w	e	f	r
z	e	h	l	a	e	y	e	s	k	l	p
w	a	y	f	i	n	g	e	r	s	c	n
b	d	m	n	q	r	u	h	l	p	q	o
w	d	g	h	m	m	o	u	t	h	y	s
d	e	a	r	s	g	t	o	e	s	y	e
g	h	a	k	n	e	e	s	l	o	p	g

body **hair**
foot **ears**
feet **toes**
head **hands**
legs **nose**
arms **mouth**
eyes **knees**
fingers

I've got 2 ________  .

I've got 2 ________  and 10 ________ 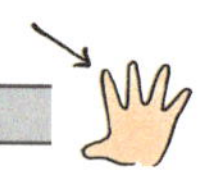 .

I see with my ________  .

I hear with my ________  .

I smell with my ________  .

I speak with my ________  .

I've got 2 ________  and 2 ________  .

This is 1 ________  and these are 2 ________ 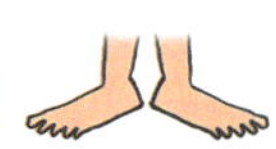 .

And I've got 10 ________ 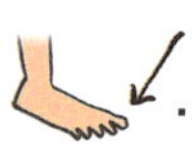 .

2. How do they feel? Draw lines and write.

How do you feel, Jack?

I'm ________________ .

I want to eat a sandwich.

How do you feel, Susan?

I'm ________________ .

It's my birthday.

How do you feel, Sam?

I'm ________________ .

I don't like spiders.

happy

sad

hungry

angry

scared

tired

fine

How do you feel, Jim?

I'm ________________ .

I broke my arm.

How do you feel, Annie?

I'm ________________ .

I can't watch TV.

How do you feel, Maggie?

I'm ________________ .

I want to go to bed.

How do you feel, Liz?

I'm ________________ , thank you.

3. Which alien is it? Read and number.

Alien number one has got two heads, five legs and three arms. It's happy.

Alien number two has got two heads, two noses and one big ear. It's angry.

Alien number three has got one head, four eyes and one mouth with two teeth.

Alien number four has got one head, five feet, one ear and one arm.

Alien number five has got __________ arms, __________ legs, __________ fingers and __________ noses.

1. What is it? Draw lines and write.

teddy bear

castle

inline skates

lorry

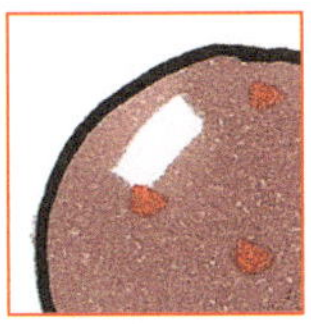

racing car

computer game

doll

helicopter

ball

spaceship

2. Do the crossword.

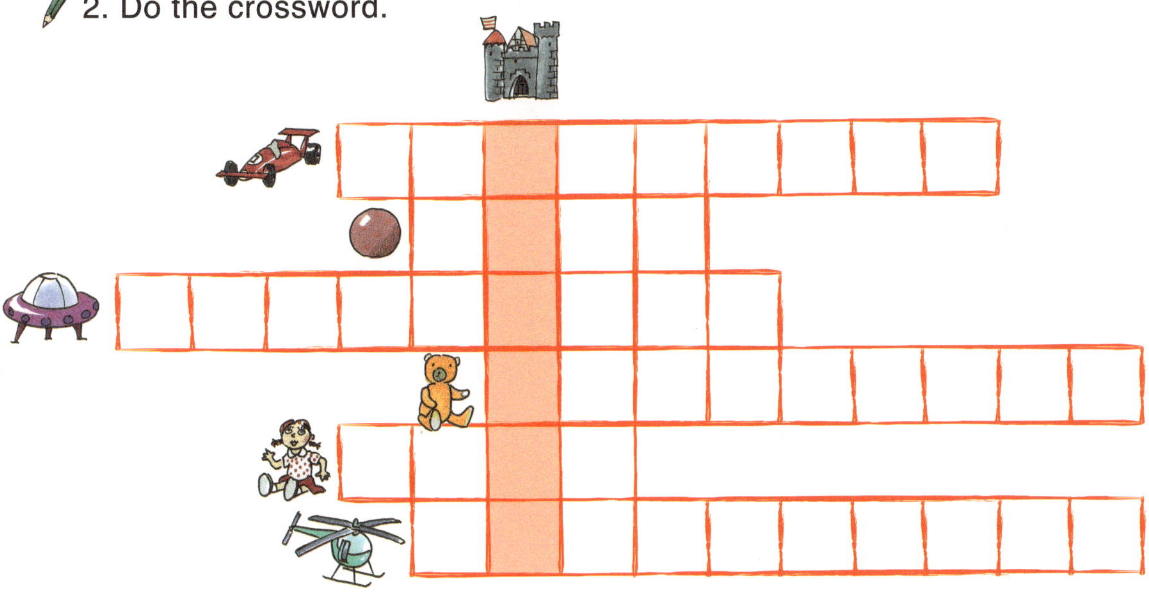

3. At the toy shop.
Match the pictures to the speech bubbles. Draw lines and fill in.

It's ________ £.

Hello, can I help you?

Thank you. Goodbye.

I like this ________________.
How much is it?

4. Trace the lines and write.

Katie buys a __________. It's _____ £.

Ken buys a __________. It's _____ £.

Anne buys a __________. It's _____ £.

Derek buys a __________. It's _____ £.

Betty buys a __________. It's _____ £.

racing car **teddy bear** **helicopter** **doll** **spaceship**

1. Such a long scarf! Find the words. Draw lines and write.

________, ________, ________,

________, ________, ________,

________ This word is missing: ________

2. Look and write.

Jenny puts on her ________ ,

her ________ 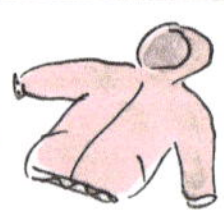

and her ________ .

Brian takes off his ________ , his

________ 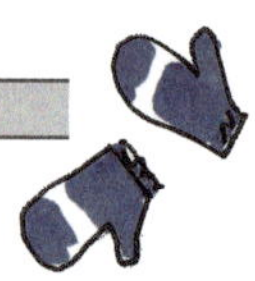 and his ________ .

shoes	**gloves**	**scarf**	**dress**	**woolly hat**	**anorak**

3. What can you see? Write.

shoes – a pullover – a skirt – a jacket

a pair of trousers – a pullover – a T-shirt – a dress

a pair of shorts – socks – a T-shirt – a pullover

4. Dress Janet and Jack. Write.

Janet: ______________________________

____

Jack: ______________________________

____

5. Funny  . Read and tick.

It's wearing…

○ a woolly hat, a jacket, a pair of trousers and shoes.

○ a cap, a scarf, a jacket, a pair of shorts and boots.

○ a cap, a scarf, an anorak, a pair of trousers and shoes.

It's wearing…

○ a woolly hat, a pullover, a pair of trousers and gloves.

○ a cap, an anorak, a T-shirt, a pair of shorts and boots.

○ a jacket, a woolly hat, socks, a pair of trousers and shoes.

It's wearing…

○ gloves, a woolly hat, a shirt, a skirt and boots.

○ gloves, a scarf, a woolly hat, a pullover and a pair of trousers.

○ a T-shirt, a dress, a cap, a pair of shorts and shoes.

Schau aus den Fenstern.
Beschreibe das Wetter.

1. Look outside the windows. What's the weather like? Write.

It's ______________ .

It's ______________

and ______________ .

snowy
hot
foggy
rainy
sunny
windy
cloudy
cold

It's ______________

and ______________ .

It's ______________

and ______________

and ______________ .

2. Odd one out.

snowy – cold – hot

sunny – cloudy – rainy

sunny – hot – snowy

windy – hot – rainy

3. Fill in the missing letters. Draw lines and write.

1. _onday
2. _uesday
3. Wednes_ _ _
4. Thursday
5. _riday
6. _atur_ _ _
7. Su_day

On Monday it's sunny.

On ______ it's ______.

On ______ it's ______.

______.

______.

______.

On ______ it's ______

and ______.

Thursday	**Monday**	**Friday**	**Tuesday**	**Saturday**	**Wednesday**
Sunday	**sunny**	**rainy**	**foggy**	**windy**	**snowy**
cloudy (2x)					

4. Read the comic.

Crazy weather

1. Draw lines and write.

mother

sister

brother

father

grandmother

grandfather

2. Look and write.

grandpa
grandma
mum
dad

3. Find the words and write. Then solve the riddles.

Mike's family tree

He's my mum's dad.
He's my grandpa.

She's my dad's sister.

She's my ____ .

She's my dad's mum.

She's my ____ .

He's my mum's brother.

He's my ____ .

4. Read and write.

My best friend has got long brown hair. She is wearing a pink pullover.

My best friend is ______________ .

My best friend is a boy. He has got short blond hair and is wearing a pair of grey shorts.

My best friend is ______________ .

My best friend has got brown hair. She likes her inline skates very much.

My best friend is ______________ .

My best friend is wearing a blue T-shirt.
He has got black hair.

My best friend is ______________ .

5. An interview. Read and fill in.

my brother Joe and
my brother Tom

my sister Helen

my friend David

Sam, 9 years

: Hello. What's your name?

: My name is ______________ .

: How old are you?

: I'm ______________ years old.

: Have you got brothers?

: Yes. I have got ______________ , Joe and Tom.

: And how many sisters have you got?

: I have got ______________ . Her name is ______________ .

: Who is your best friend?

: My best ______________ is ______________ .

Trage zu jedem Wort die richtige Nummer ein und spure nach.

1. Number and write.

- ◯ hot chocolate
- ◯ coffee
- ◯ tea
- ◯ orange juice
- ◯ milk
- ◯ coke
- ◯ lemonade
- ◯ water
- ◯ apple juice

2. Look at the pictures. Find the words and circle them. What's missing?

Finde die Wörter. Die Bilder helfen dir. Ein Bild bleibt übrig. Welches Wort fehlt? Schreibe es auf.

This word is missing: ____________________

3. Look and write.

My favourite drink is ____.

My favourite drink is ____.

My favourite drink is ____.

My favourite drink is ____.

My favourite drink is ____.

My favourite drink is ____.

My favourite drink is ____ ____.

My favourite drink is ____ ____.

My favourite drink is ____ ____.

hot chocolate   coffee   tea   orange juice   milk
coke   lemonade   water   apple juice

1. Look and write.

cornflakes honey bacon egg jam roll butter
bread toast ham

2. Find the words and write.

r  ll

b  n

e 

corn  s

ho  y

Informationen für Eltern und Lehrkräfte

Englisch spielerisch üben mit den Englisch-Stars

Aufbau und Gestaltung der Englisch-Stars

Mit den Englisch-Stars üben und sichern die Kinder auf spielerische Weise den für die Grundschule wichtigen Wortschatz sowie ihr Lese- und Schreibvermögen. Abwechslungsreiche Übungsformen und ansprechende Illustrationen motivieren, Wörter und Strukturen vielfältig anzuwenden.

Das Känguru Sally ist dabei ständiger Begleiter. Die beiden deutschsprachigen Kinder Lisa und Max unterstützen mit Tipps und Hilfestellungen.

Die Englisch-Stars sind unterteilt in verschiedene Themenbereiche, die unabhängig voneinander bearbeitet werden können. Zusätzlich bieten sie im Anhang ein kleines Picture dictionary (Bildwörterbuch). Zu jedem Thema gibt es dort eine Seite, die den Wortschatz einführt. Daher ist es empfehlenswert, diese jeweils als Erstes zu bearbeiten.

Im Anschluss folgen vielfältige Übungen zur Wortschatzwiederholung und -sicherung sowie zur Sicherung des Lese- und Schreibvermögens, z.B. Zuordnungsaufgaben, Bilderrätsel und Dialoge. Lustige Comics mit Sally zeigen den Kindern, wie viel sie schon selbstständig lesen und verstehen können.
Eindeutige Aufgabenstellungen und Selbstkontrolle durch den Lösungsteil ermöglichen den Kindern, eigenständig mit den Englisch-Stars zu arbeiten.

Für jede Seite im Picture dictionary, nach jedem Thema und für besonders schwierige Aufgaben (Sternchenaufgaben) dürfen sich die Kinder mit einem Sternchen-Aufkleber belohnen. Als besonderer Anreiz ergeben die Sterne am Ende des Heftes ein Gesamtbild.

Die Englisch-Stars dienen der spielerischen und zwanglosen Auseinandersetzung mit Englisch und fördern die Freude am Erlernen der Fremdsprache.

Achtung: Die Lösung zur Seite 3 findest du ganz hinten.

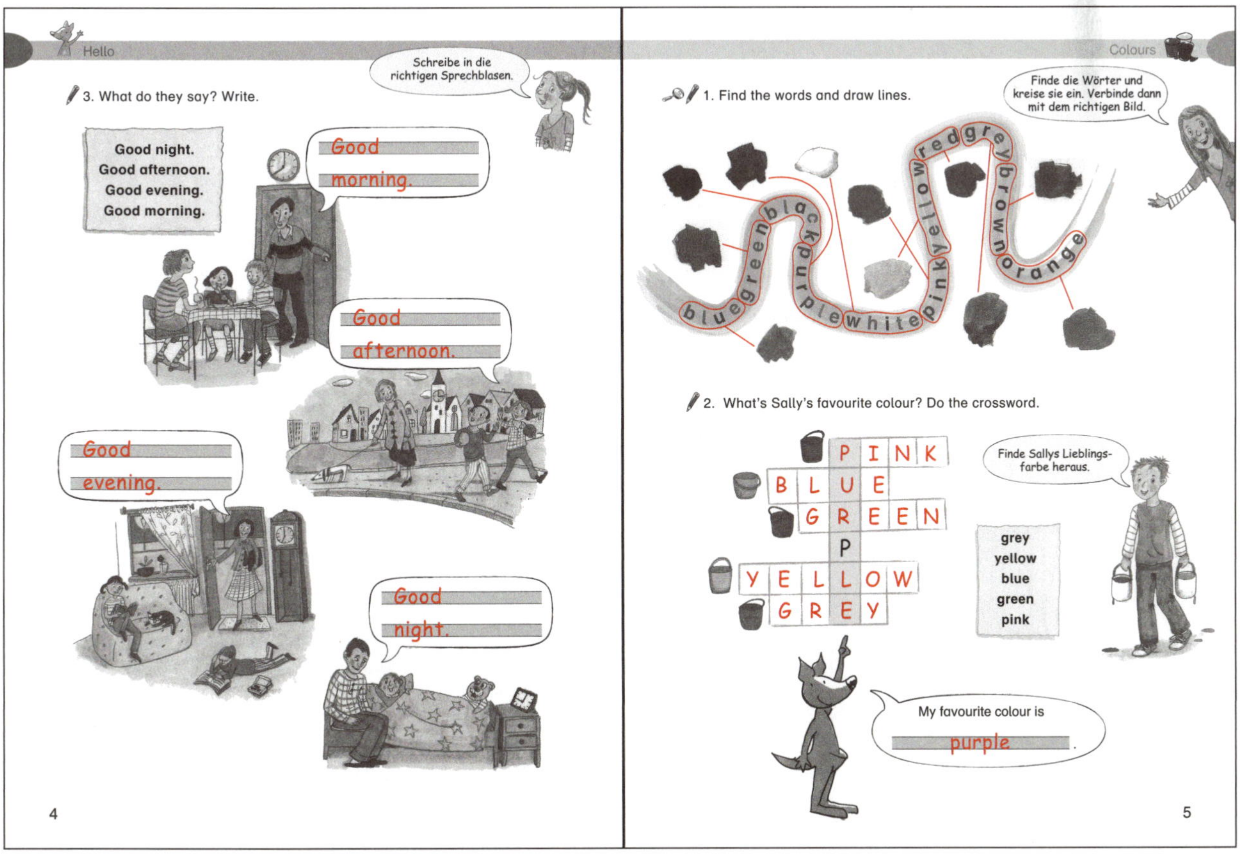

Verbinde mit den richtigen Farben. Achtung, zu zwei Bildern gehören mehrere Farben.

3. Draw lines.

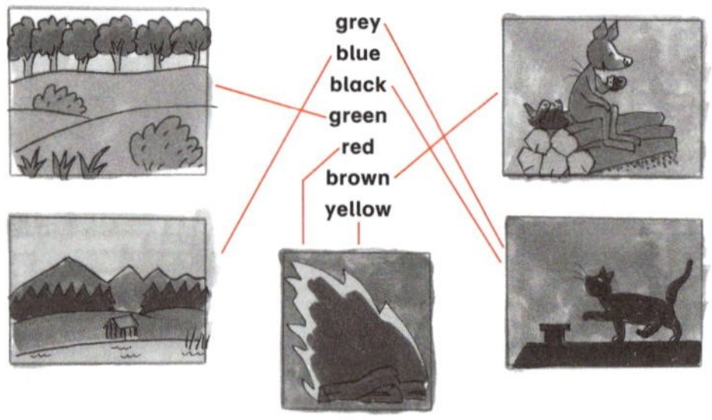

4. Write and colour.

purple – rruppe
white – hiwet
green – energ
red – edr
grey – ryge
yellow – llwyoe

yellow
green
white
red
purple
grey

Was soll das denn heißen?

Da sind Buchstaben durcheinandergekommen. Schreibe erst das Wort, male dann den Pinsel in der richtigen Farbe an.

5. Find the words and circle them.

y	m	a	b	j	l	g
e	o	g	r	e	e	n
l	r	g	o	h	b	h
l	a	e	w	d	l	a
o	n	a	n	v	u	u
w	g	a	g	r	e	y
r	e	d	c	u	k	p
f	g	n	i	z	h	u
o	b	w	h	i	t	e

Suche die Wörter senkrecht und waagrecht. Kreise ein.

orange	brown
green	yellow
red	white
grey	blue

6. What colour is missing? Write.

Welche Farben fehlen? Schreibe die Wörter in der richtigen Farbe dazu.

red + blue = purple

yellow + blue = green

yellow + red = orange

black + white = grey

1. Write the numbers in the correct order.

one, two, three, four,
five, six, seven, eight,
nine, ten

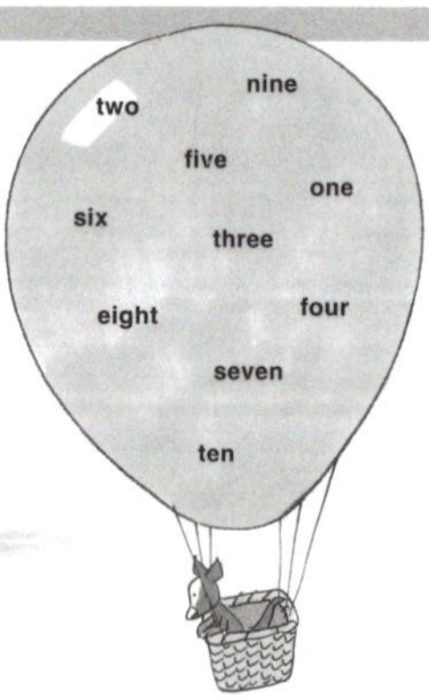

Da sollen wir bestimmt die Zahlen in der richtigen Reihenfolge aufschreiben.

2. Count and write.

Wie viele Fische gibt es von jeder Art?

eight three five six

Oh, was ist denn hier passiert? Aber du kannst das Wort sicher noch einmal richtig aufschreiben.

3. Do you know the word? Write.

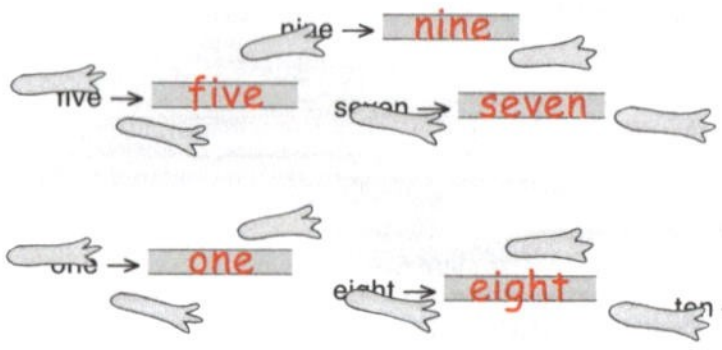

4. How many lollies? Trace the lines and write.

Fahre die Linien nach. Wie viele Lollis bekommt jeder? Schreibe die Zahlen als Wörter.

ten lollies

four lollies

six lollies

eight lollies

5. How much is it? Write.

three + one = four
ten – seven = three
two + five = seven
five – four = one
three + six = nine
seven – five = two
four + one = five
nine – eight = one

6. Correct or wrong? Tick.

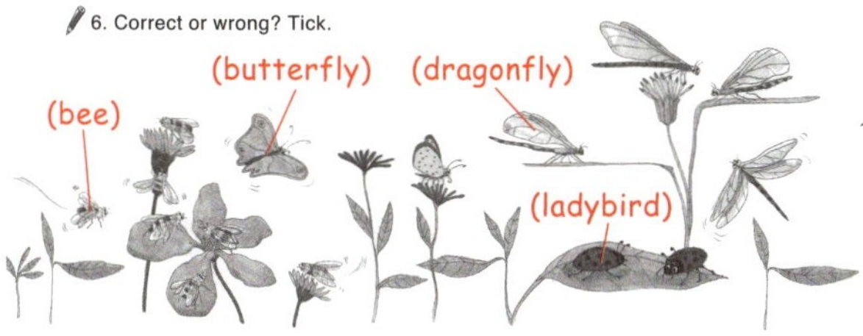

	correct	wrong
There are **two** (ladybird).	✓	
There is **one** (dragonfly).		✓
There are **eight** (butterfly).		✓
There are **seven** (bee).	✓	

1. Number.

1 schoolbag
2 book
3 folder
4 ruler
5 pencil case
6 pencil
7 rubber
8 scissors
9 glue

2. Draw lines.

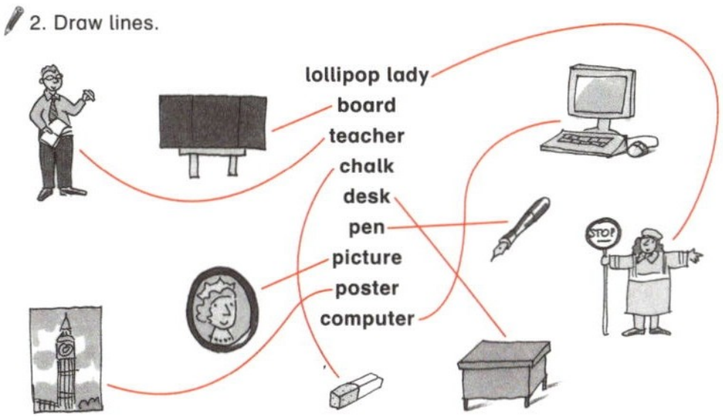

3. Odd one out.

rubber – ruler – ~~girl~~ – computer
pen – scissors – pencil – ~~song~~
board – chalk – ~~five~~ – desk
~~book~~ – boy – teacher – pupil

4. Read, look and write. What's missing?

What's missing on Steve's desk?
The pencil is missing.

What's missing on Kathy's desk?
The rubber is missing.

What's missing on Polly's desk?
The folder is missing.

5. Read and colour.

The pencil case is green.
The ruler is yellow.
The pen is red.
The pencil is blue.
The rubber is pink.
The lollipop is purple.

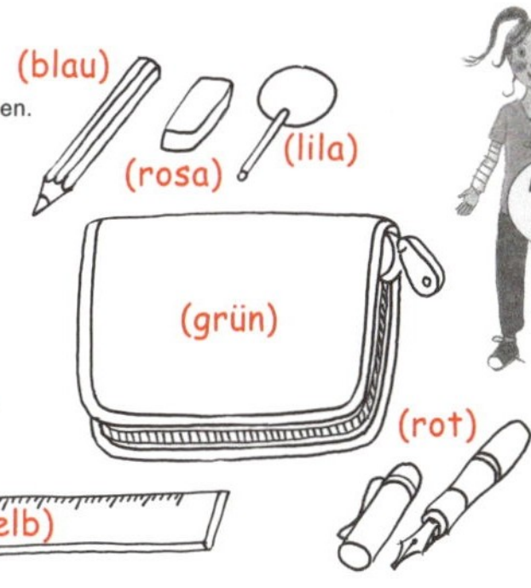

6. What belongs into the schoolbag? Write.

pencil, ruler, scissors, pencil case, desk, chalk, board, poster, folder, pen, glue, rubber, computer, book

book, folder, glue, pen, pencil,
pencil case, rubber, ruler,
scissors

Lösungen

1. Find the words and circle them. Fill in.

n	b	o	d	y	t	u	r	z	l	u	q
s	h	a	n	d	s	x	c	b	e	l	v
f	a	w	a	r	m	s	p	y	g	m	h
e	s	q	r	b	m	l	o	p	s	y	a
e	c	v	e	f	o	o	t	a	b	u	i
t	h	y	b	t	j	k	h	w	e	f	r
z	e	h	l	a	e	y	e	s	k	l	p
w	a	y	f	i	n	g	e	r	s	c	n
b	d	m	n	q	r	u	h	l	p	q	o
w	d	g	h	m	m	o	u	t	h	y	s
d	e	a	r	s	g	t	o	e	s	y	e
g	h	a	k	n	e	e	s	l	o	p	g

body	hair
foot	ears
feet	toes
head	hands
legs	nose
arms	mouth
eyes	knees
fingers	

I've got 2 arms.

I've got 2 hands and 10 fingers.

I see with my eyes.

I hear with my ears.

I smell with my nose.

I speak with my mouth.

I've got 2 legs and 2 knees.

This is 1 foot and these are 2 feet.

And I've got 10 toes.

2. How do they feel? Draw lines and write.

happy · sad · hungry · angry · scared · tired · fine

How do you feel, Jack?

I'm hungry.

I want to eat a sandwich.

How do you feel, Jim?

I'm sad.

I broke my arm.

How do you feel, Susan?

I'm happy.

It's my birthday.

How do you feel, Annie?

I'm angry.

I can't watch TV.

How do you feel, Sam?

I'm scared.

I don't like spiders.

How do you feel, Maggie?

I'm tired.

I want to go to bed.

How do you feel, Liz?

I'm fine, thank you.

3. Which alien is it? Read and number.

Alien number one has got two heads, five legs and three arms.
It's happy.

Alien number two has got two heads, two noses and one big ear.
It's angry.

Alien number three has got one head, four eyes and one mouth with two teeth.

Alien number four has got one head, five feet, one ear and one arm.

Alien number five has got four arms, three legs, four fingers and two noses.

1. What is it? Draw lines and write.

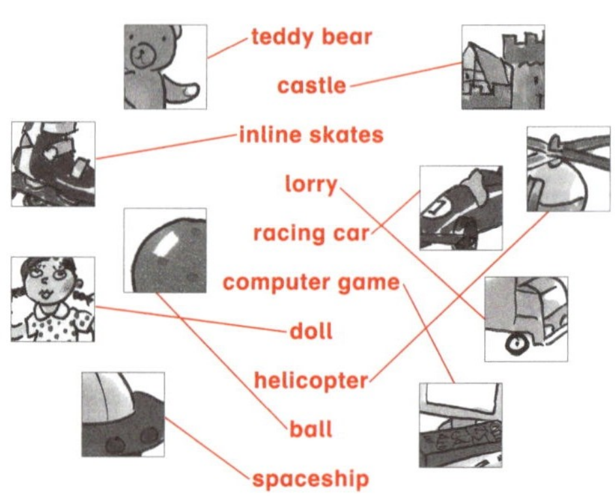

2. Do the crossword.

			R	A	C	I	N	G	C	A	R		
				B	A	L	L						
S	P	A	C	E	S	H	I	P					
					T	E	D	D	Y	B	E	A	R
			D	O	L	L							
				H	E	L	I	C	O	P	T	E	R

Jetzt kannst du schon auf Englisch rechnen. Schreibe die Ergebnisse als Wörter.

5. How much is it? Write.

three + one = four
ten – seven = three
two + five = seven
five – four = one
three + six = nine
seven – five = two
four + one = five
nine – eight = one

6. Correct or wrong? Tick.

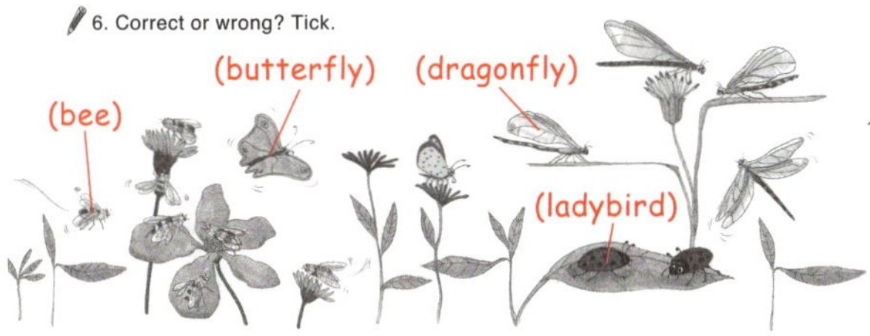

Richtig oder falsch? Mache einen Haken.

	correct	wrong
There are **two** (ladybird).	✓	
There is **one** (dragonfly).		✓
There are **eight** (butterfly).		✓
There are **seven** (bee).	✓	

1. Number.

Ordne den Schulsachen die richtige Zahl zu.

1 schoolbag
2 book
3 folder
4 ruler
5 pencil case
6 pencil
7 rubber
8 scissors
9 glue

2. Draw lines.

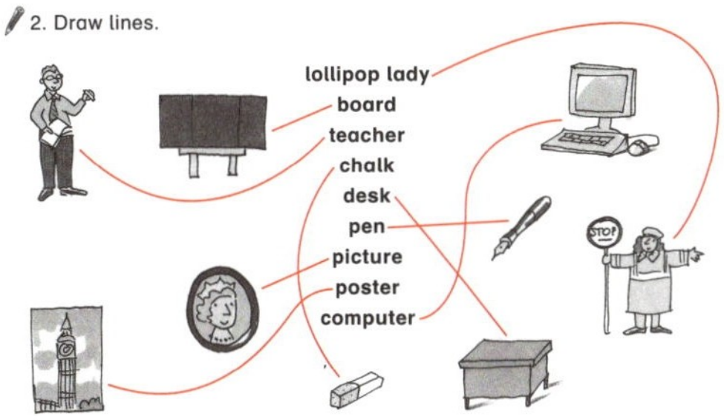

3. Odd one out.

Jeweils ein Wort in der Reihe passt nicht. Streiche es durch.

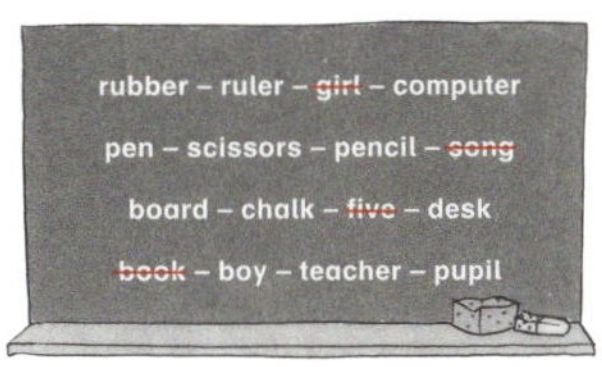

4. Read, look and write. What's missing?

Was sollen die Kinder alles aus ihrer Schultasche nehmen? Auf jedem Tisch fehlt etwas.

Take out your folder, a pencil, a rubber, glue and scissors.

What's missing on Steve's desk?
The pencil is missing.

What's missing on Kathy's desk?
The rubber is missing.

What's missing on Polly's desk?
The folder is missing.

5. Read and colour.

The pencil case is green.
The ruler is yellow.
The pen is red.
The pencil is blue.
The rubber is pink.
The lollipop is purple.

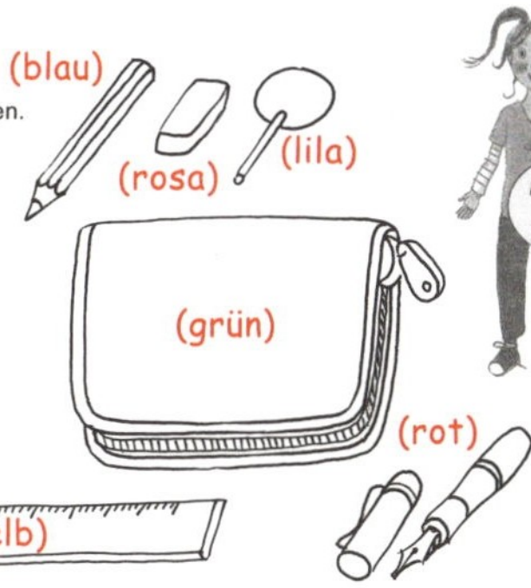

Male in der richtigen Farbe aus.

6. What belongs into the schoolbag? Write.

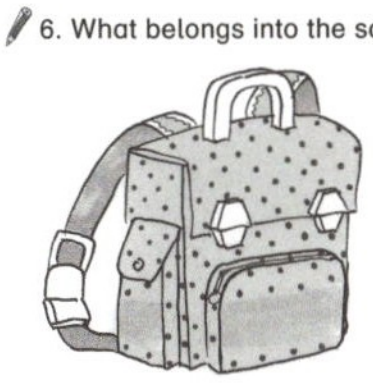

pencil, ruler, scissors, pencil case, desk, chalk, board, poster, folder, pen, glue, rubber, computer, book

book, folder, glue, pen, pencil,
pencil case, rubber, ruler,
scissors

Schreibe auf, was in die Schultasche gehört.

Lösungen

Finde die Wörter senkrecht und waagrecht. Kreise sie ein. Trage sie dann unten richtig ein.

1. Find the words and circle them. Fill in.

n	b	o	d	y	t	u	r	z	l	u	q
s	h	a	n	d	s	x	c	b	e	l	v
f	a	w	a	r	m	s	p	y	g	m	h
e	s	q	r	b	m	l	o	p	s	y	a
e	c	v	e	f	o	o	t	a	b	u	i
t	h	y	b	t	j	k	h	w	e	f	r
z	e	h	l	a	e	y	e	s	k	l	p
w	a	y	f	i	n	g	e	r	s	c	n
b	d	m	n	q	r	u	h	l	p	q	o
w	d	g	h	m	m	o	u	t	h	y	s
d	e	a	r	s	g	t	o	e	s	y	e
g	h	a	k	n	e	e	s	l	o	p	g

body	hair
foot	ears
feet	toes
head	hands
legs	nose
arms	mouth
eyes	knees
fingers	

I've got 2 arms.

I've got 2 hands and 10 fingers.

I see with my eyes.

I hear with my ears.

I smell with my nose.

I speak with my mouth.

I've got 2 legs and 2 knees.

This is 1 foot and these are 2 feet.

And I've got 10 toes.

2. How do they feel? Draw lines and write.

How do you feel, Jack?

I'm hungry.

I want to eat a sandwich.

How do you feel, Susan?

I'm happy.

It's my birthday.

How do you feel, Sam?

I'm scared.

I don't like spiders.

happy
sad
hungry
angry
scared
tired
fine

How do you feel, Jim?

I'm sad.

I broke my arm.

How do you feel, Annie?

I'm angry.

I can't watch TV.

How do you feel, Maggie?

I'm tired.

I want to go to bed.

How do you feel, Liz?

I'm fine, thank you.

3. Which alien is it? Read and number.

Alien number one has got two heads, five legs and three arms. It's happy.

Alien number two has got two heads, two noses and one big ear. It's angry.

Alien number three has got one head, four eyes and one mouth with two teeth.

Alien number four has got one head, five feet, one ear and one arm.

Alien number five has got four arms, three legs, four fingers and two noses.

1. What is it? Draw lines and write.

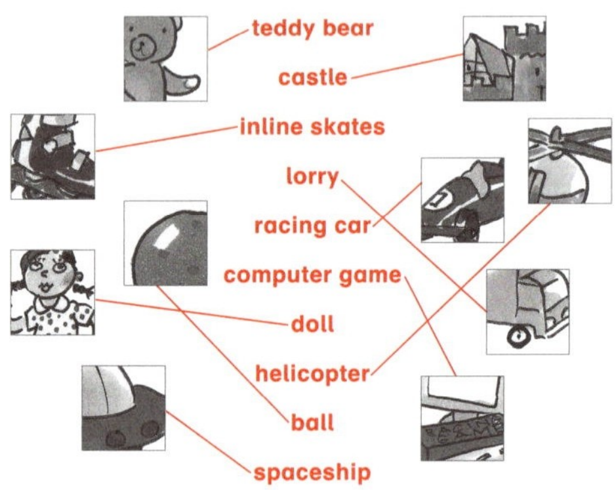

2. Do the crossword.

3. At the toy shop.
Match the pictures to the speech bubbles. Draw lines and fill in.

4. Trace the lines and write.

Katie buys a doll. It's 4 (four) £.

Ken buys a racing car. It's 8 (eight) £.

Anne buys a spaceship. It's 6 (six) £.

Derek buys a helicopter. It's 10 (ten) £.

Betty buys a teddy bear. It's 5 (five) £.

racing car teddy bear helicopter doll spaceship

1. Such a long scarf! Find the words. Draw lines and write.

skirt, trousers, pullover,
boots, cap, socks,
shirt This word is missing: T-shirt

2. Look and write.

Jenny puts on her dress,
her anorak
and her shoes.
Brian takes off his woolly hat, his
gloves and his scarf.

shoes gloves scarf dress woolly hat anorak

3. What can you see? Write.

shoes – a pullover – a skirt – a jacket

a pair of trousers – a pullover – a T-shirt – a dress

a pair of shorts – socks – a T-shirt – a pullover

4. Dress Janet and Jack. Write.

(mögliche Lösung)

Janet: a skirt, a T-Shirt, socks, (pink) shoes, a woolly hat, a scarf, a jacket

Jack: a pair of trousers, a shirt, gloves, a cap, a pullover, (brown) shoes, an anorak, socks

5. Funny scarecrows. Read and tick.

It's wearing...
- ◯ a woolly hat, a jacket, a pair of trousers and shoes.
- ✓ a cap, a scarf, a jacket, a pair of shorts and boots.
- ◯ a cap, a scarf, an anorak, a pair of trousers and shoes.

It's wearing...
- ◯ a woolly hat, a pullover, a pair of trousers and gloves.
- ◯ a cap, an anorak, a T-shirt, a pair of shorts and boots.
- ✓ a jacket, a woolly hat, socks, a pair of trousers and shoes.

It's wearing...
- ✓ gloves, a woolly hat, a shirt, a skirt and boots.
- ◯ gloves, a scarf, a woolly hat, a pullover and a pair of trousers.
- ◯ a T-shirt, a dress, a cap, a pair of shorts and shoes.

☆

Schau aus den Fenstern. Beschreibe das Wetter.

1. Look outside the windows. What's the weather like? Write.

snowy
hot
foggy
rainy
sunny
windy
cloudy
cold

It's **foggy**.

It's **sunny** and **hot**.

It's **snowy** and **cold**.

It's **cloudy** and **windy** and **rainy**.

2. Odd one out.

snowy – cold – ~~hot~~

~~sunny~~ – cloudy – rainy

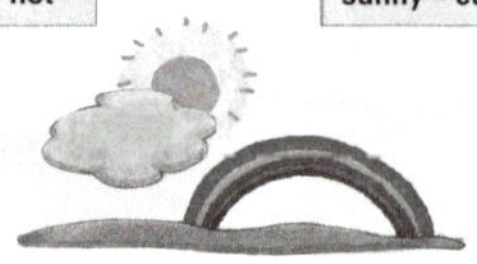

sunny – hot – ~~snowy~~

windy – ~~hot~~ – rainy

3. Fill in the missing letters. Draw lines and write.

Ergänze zuerst die fehlenden Buchstaben der Wochentage. Verbinde dann die Wochentage mit den passenden Bildern und schreibe auf.

1. **M**onday
2. **T**uesday
3. Wednes**day**
4. Thursday
5. **F**riday
6. **S**atur**day**
7. Su**n**day

On Monday it's sunny.

On **Tuesday** it's **foggy**.

On **Wednesday** it's **windy**.

On Thursday it's snowy.

On Friday it's rainy.

On Saturday it's cloudy.

On **Sunday** it's **cloudy** and **rainy**.

☆

Thursday	Monday	Friday	Tuesday	Saturday	Wednesday
Sunday	sunny	rainy	foggy	windy	snowy	cloudy (2x)

4. Read the comic.

Crazy weather

1. Draw lines and write.

mother, sister, brother, father,
grandmother, grandfather

2. Look and write.

mum

dad

grandpa
grandma
mum
dad

grandma

grandpa

3. Find the words and write. Then solve the riddles.

Mike's family tree

He's my mum's dad.
He's my grandpa.

She's my dad's sister.
She's my a u n t .

She's my dad's mum.
She's my g r a n d m a .

He's my mum's brother.
He's my u n c l e .

4. Read and write.

My best friend has got long brown hair. She is wearing a pink pullover.
My best friend is Lucy .

My best friend is a boy. He has got short blond hair and is wearing a pair of grey shorts.
My best friend is Ben .

My best friend has got brown hair. She likes her inline skates very much.
My best friend is Anna .

My best friend is wearing a blue T-shirt. He has got black hair.
My best friend is John .

5. An interview. Read and fill in.

my brother Joe and my brother Tom

my sister Helen

my friend David

Sam, 9 years

: Hello. What's your name?

: My name is Sam .

: How old are you?

: I'm nine years old.

: Have you got brothers?

: Yes. I have got two brothers , Joe and Tom.

: And how many sisters have you got?

: I have got one sister . Her name is Helen .

: Who is your best friend?

: My best friend is David .

1. Number and write.

(3) hot chocolate
(8) coffee
(2) tea
(9) orange juice
(4) milk
(6) coke
(5) lemonade
(1) water
(7) apple juice

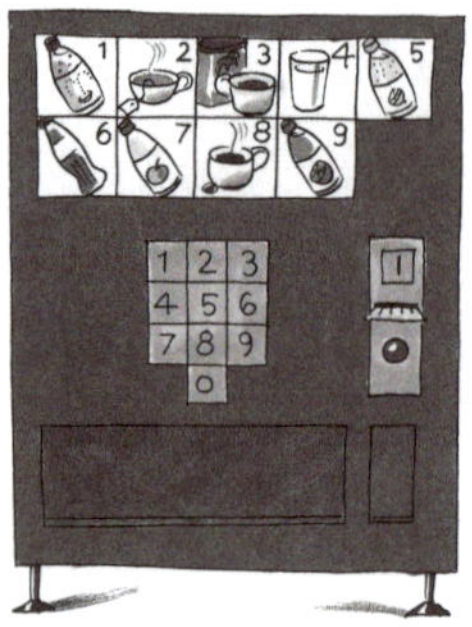

2. Look at the pictures. Find the words and circle them. What's missing?

This word is missing: orange juice

3. Look and write.

My favourite drink is coke.
My favourite drink is lemonade.
My favourite drink is coffee.

My favourite drink is milk.
My favourite drink is water.
My favourite drink is tea.

My favourite drink is orange juice.
My favourite drink is apple juice.
My favourite drink is hot chocolate.

hot chocolate coffee tea orange juice milk coke lemonade water apple juice

1. Look and write.

cornflakes honey bacon egg jam roll butter bread toast ham

2. Find the words and write.

r__ll — roll
b__n — bacon
e__ — egg
corn__s — cornflakes
ho__y — honey

3. Read and draw lines.

4. What's missing? Read and draw.

1 2 3 5. Read and number.

Findest du heraus, wer an welchem Platz sitzt?

I don't like cornflakes, but I like coffee. (2)

I like toast, but I don't like hot chocolate. (3)

I don't like toast. (1)

I don't like ham. (4)

6. Crazy breakfast. What's wrong? Write.

Irgendwie sind die Sätze durcheinandergeraten. Schreibe sie richtig auf.

I like a roll with tea and a cup of jam.

I like a roll with jam and a cup of tea.

I like toast with cornflakes and honey with milk.

I like toast with honey and cornflakes with milk.

I like bread with orange juice and a glass of ham.

I like bread with ham and a glass of orange juice.

1. Do the crossword.

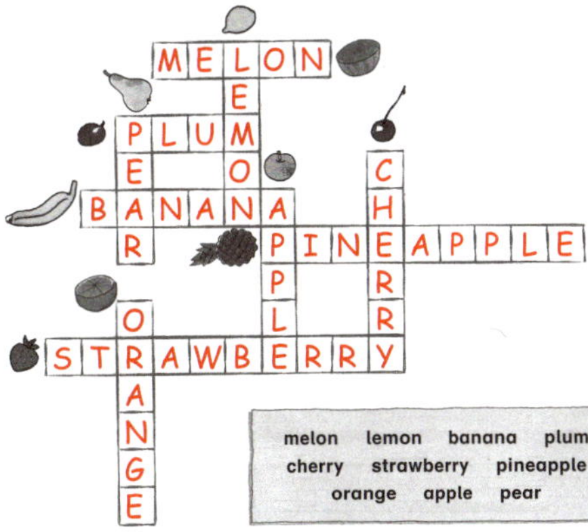

melon lemon banana plum cherry strawberry pineapple orange apple pear

2. Find the five fruit in the basket. Write.

banana

lemon

melon

pear

pineapple

3. Trace the lines and write.

Wörter mit -y am Ende schreibe ich in der Mehrzahl mit -ies. Wie bei cherry – cherries.

Dave likes plums.

Sarah likes strawberries.

Emily likes oranges.

Tim likes apples.

Mary likes cherries.

strawberries cherries apples plums oranges

4. Guess the fruit and write.

banana pear melon apple

5. Read the comic.

Yummy fruit juices

1. What pet is it? Write and draw lines.

budgie	cat
dog	fish
guinea pig	
hamster	mouse
rabbit	tortoise

My pet is red. It can swim.
It's a fish.

My pet is black. It says "miaow".
It's a cat.

My pet is blue. It can fly.
It's a budgie.

My pet is brown and white. It's very small.
It's a hamster.

My pet is brown. It says "bow-wow".
It's a dog.

My pet is black and white. It likes apples.
It's a guinea pig.

My pet is green. It has got short legs.
It's a tortoise.

My pet is white. It has got long ears.
It's a rabbit.

2. Find the pets and colour the fields green. What can you see?

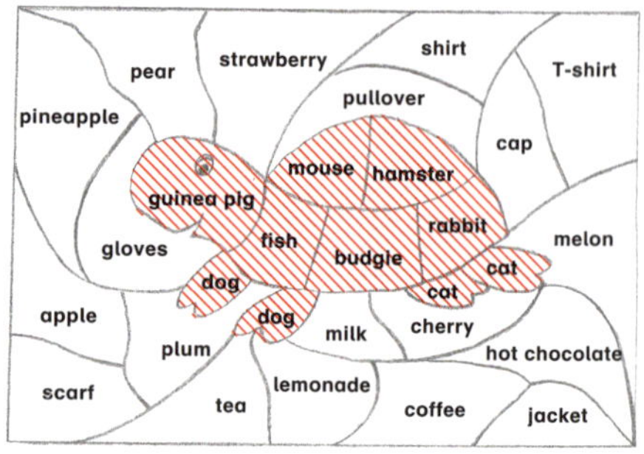

I can see a tortoise.

3. Guess the pets. Write.

rabbit, cat, mouse, dog

4. Trace the lines and write.

A dog likes (ham).
A cat likes (fish).
A rabbit likes (carrots).
A guinea pig likes (apples).
A mouse likes (cheese).

mouse
cat
guinea pig
dog
rabbit

1. Write and draw lines.

spring	summer
autumn	winter

May
April
March

It's spring.

June
August
July

It's summer.

September
November
October

It's autumn.

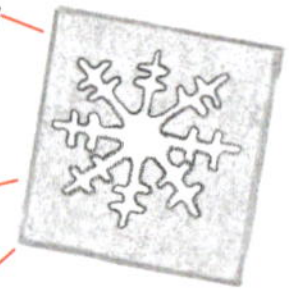

January
February
December

It's winter.

2. Write the 12 months in the correct order.

1. January	2. February	3. March
4. April	5. May	6. June
7. July	8. August	9. September
10. October	11. November	12. December

3. Read and tick the correct answer.

Easter is in ...
- ○ winter ○ summer ✓ spring.

Christmas is in ...
- ✓ December ○ November ○ September.

Halloween is in ...
- ○ April ✓ October ○ February.

The summer holidays are in ...
- ○ January ○ March ✓ July/August.

4. What can you see? Write.

pond · butter-fly · tree · grass · frog · flower

I can see a **tree** .

I can see a **flower** .

I can see a **frog** .

I can see a **pond** .

I can see **grass** .

I can see a **butterfly** .

5. Find the months. Draw lines and write.

Octo- · Novem- · Jul- · Janua- · Mar- · -ber · Decem- · Septem-

Welche dieser Monate haben die Endung -ber.

September, October, November, December

6. What can you see?
Colour the spring words green, the summer words yellow, the autumn words brown and the winter words blue.

Male die Frühlingswörter grün, die Sommerwörter gelb, die Herbstwörter braun und die Winterwörter blau an. Und dann lass dich überraschen.

blau
gelb
braun
grün

I can see a ______________ .

1. These animals live on a farm. Write the words and draw lines.

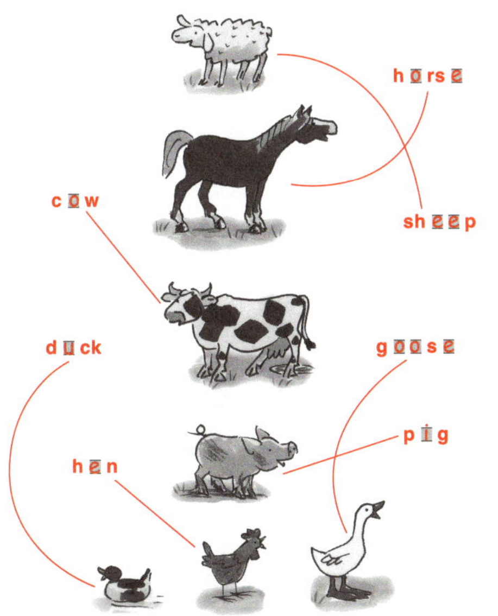

horse pig hen sheep goose cow duck

2. What do they say? Write.

Was ist denn hier passiert? Wie muss es richtig heißen? Trage in die Lücken ein.

A **duck** says quak-quak.

A **hen** says cluck-cluck.

A **pig** says oink-oink.

A **horse** says neigh-neigh.

A **goose** says honk-honk.

A **sheep** says baa-baa.

A **cow** says moo-moo.

duck goose horse pig hen sheep cow

3. Read the comic.

On the farm

1. Colour the British flag – The Union Jack.

2. What can you see in the pictures? Write.

Tower Bridge

London Eye

Buckingham Palace

Big Ben

Buckingham Palace	**Tower Bridge**	**London Eye**	**Big Ben**

3. Read the comic.

Sally in London

morning
afternoon
evening
night

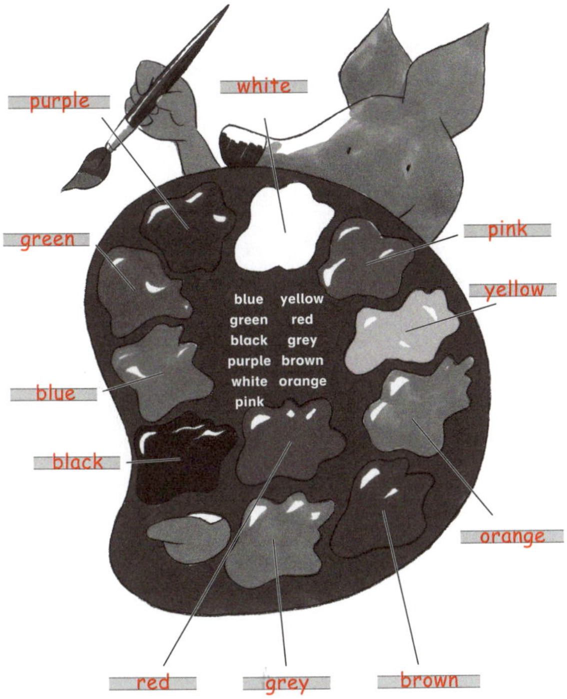

one two three four five six seven
eight nine ten

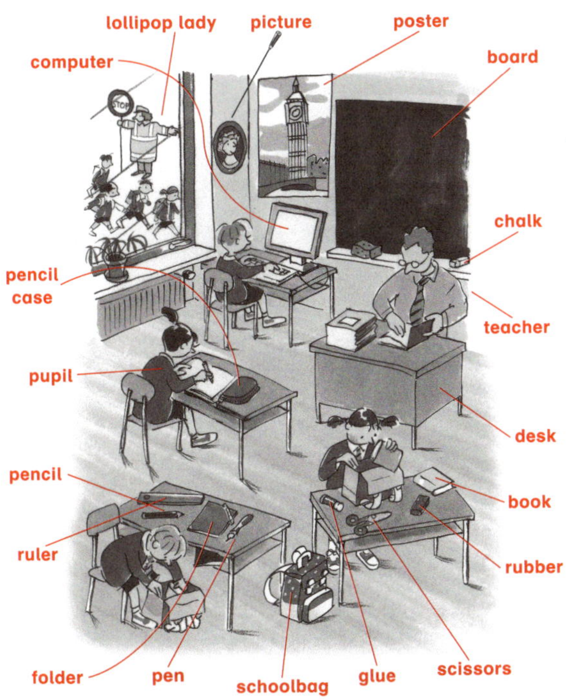

arms ears hands legs fingers toes
nose eyes tooth/teeth foot/feet knees

racing car	doll	computer game	castle	spaceship
ball	helicopter	lorry	inline skates	teddy bear

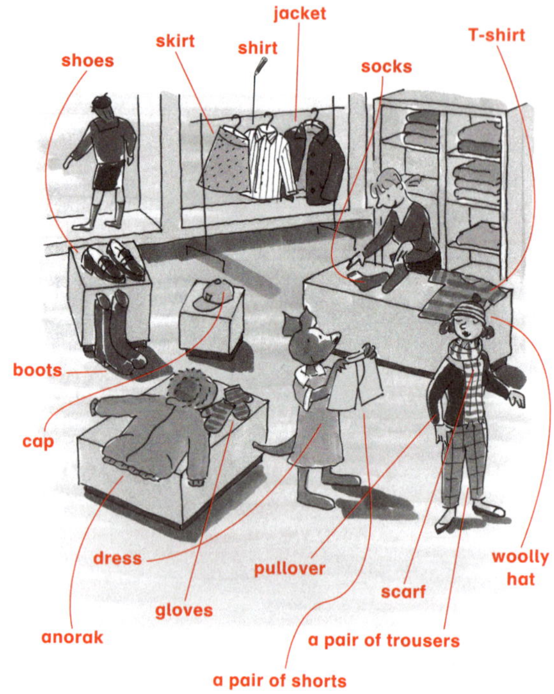

It's windy.

It's foggy.

It's rainy.

It's cloudy.

It's sunny and hot.

It's snowy and cold.

sunny	rainy	snowy
cloudy	foggy	windy
cold	hot	

grandmother/grandma	aunt	father	uncle	sister
mother	dad	brother	mum	grandfather/ grandpa

hot chocolate coffee
tea milk coke
orange juice lemonade
water apple juice

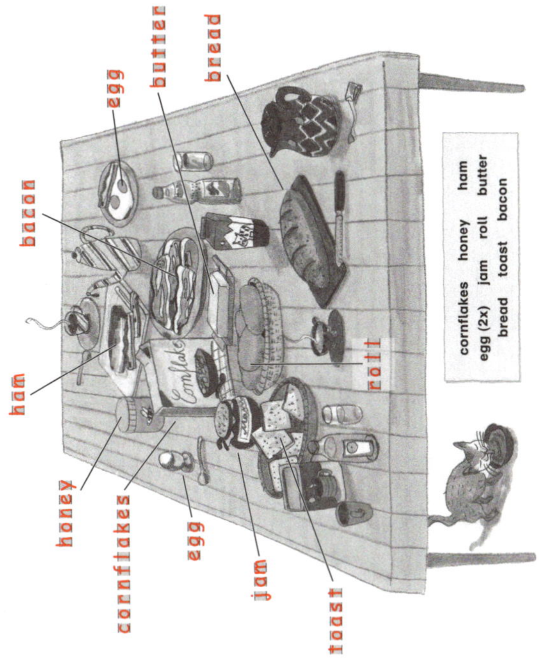

cornflakes honey ham
egg (2x) jam roll butter
bread toast bacon

melon lemon banana
plum cherry orange
strawberry pear
apple pineapple

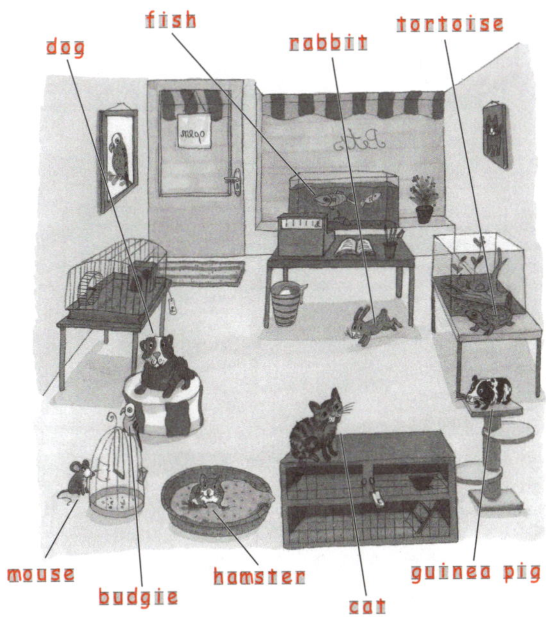

budgie tortoise hamster cat guinea pig dog
rabbit mouse fish

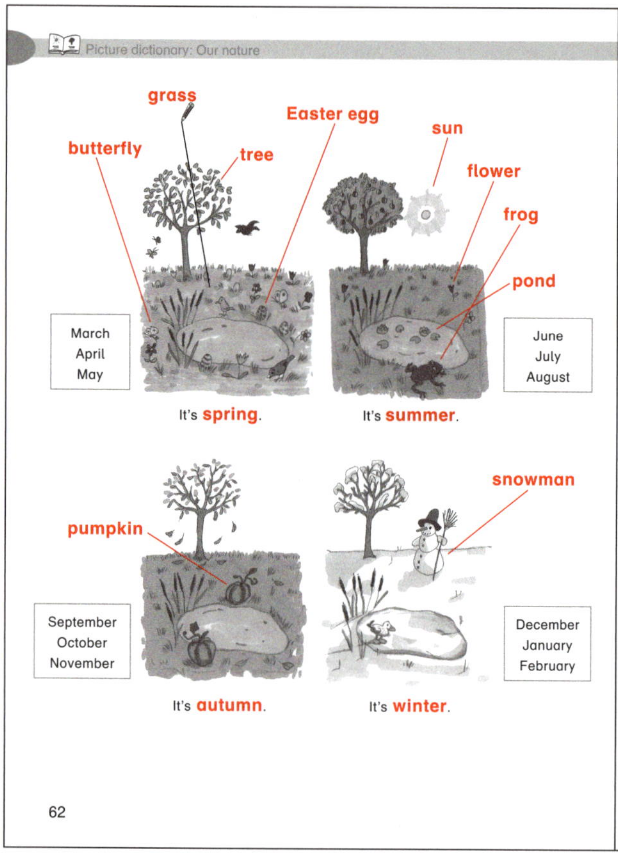

Die Lösung zur Seite 3:

3. Read and draw lines.

4. What's missing? Read and draw.

5. Read and number.

 I don't like cornflakes, but I like coffee. ◯

 I like toast, but I don't like hot chocolate. ◯

 I don't like toast. ◯

 I don't like ham. ◯

6. Crazy breakfast. What's wrong? Write.

 I like a roll with tea and a cup of jam.

____

 I like toast with cornflakes and honey with milk.

____

 I like bread with orange juice and a glass of ham.

____

1. Do the crossword.

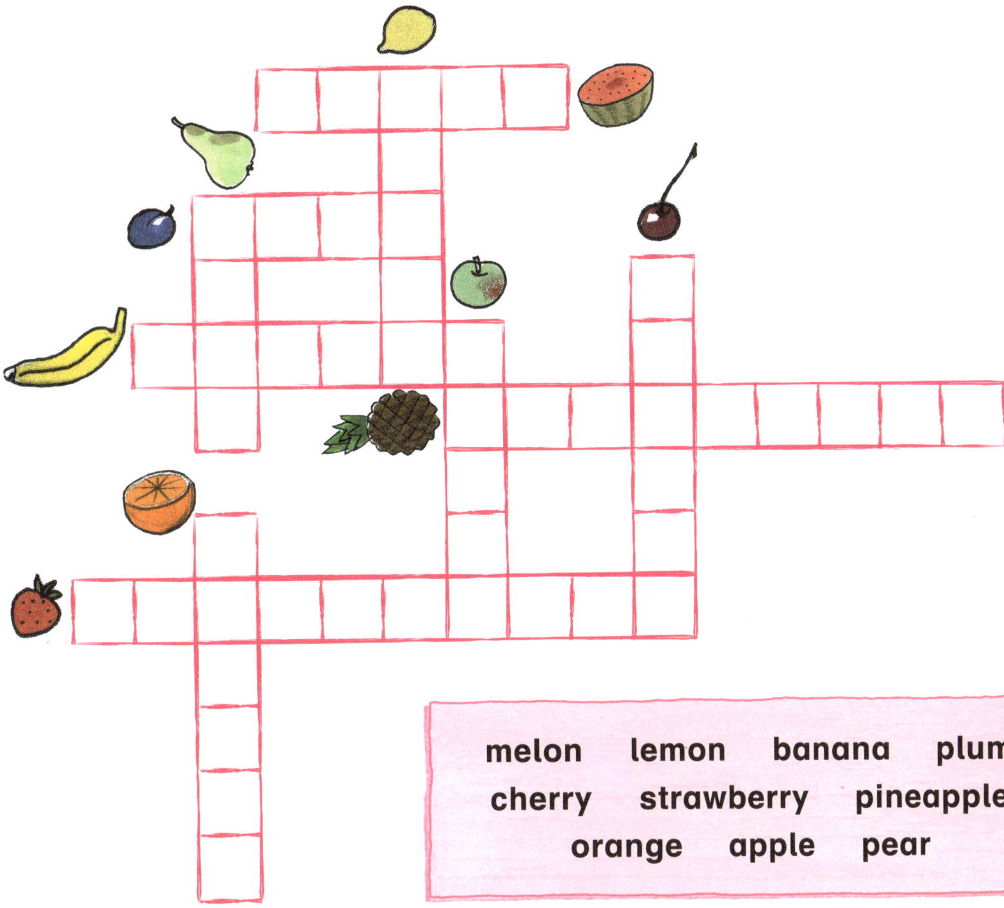

melon lemon banana plum
cherry strawberry pineapple
orange apple pear

2. Find the five fruit in the basket. Write.

3. Trace the lines and write.

__________ likes plums.

__________ likes __________ .

__________ likes __________ .

__________ likes __________ .

__________ likes __________ .

strawberries **cherries** **apples** **plums** **oranges**

4. Guess the fruit and write.

banana
pear
melon
apple

5. Read the comic.

Yummy fruit juices

1. What pet is it? Write and draw lines.

budgie **cat**
dog **fish**
guinea pig
hamster **mouse**
rabbit **tortoise**

My pet is red. It can swim.
It's a ______________ .

My pet is black. It says "miaow".
It's a ______________ .

My pet is blue. It can fly.
It's a ______________ .

My pet is brown and white. It's very small.
It's a ______________ .

My pet is brown. It says "bow-wow".
It's a ______________ .

My pet is black and white. It likes apples.
It's a ______________ .

My pet is green. It has got short legs.
It's a ______________ .

My pet is white. It has got long ears.
It's a ______________ .

2. Find the pets and colour the fields green. What can you see?

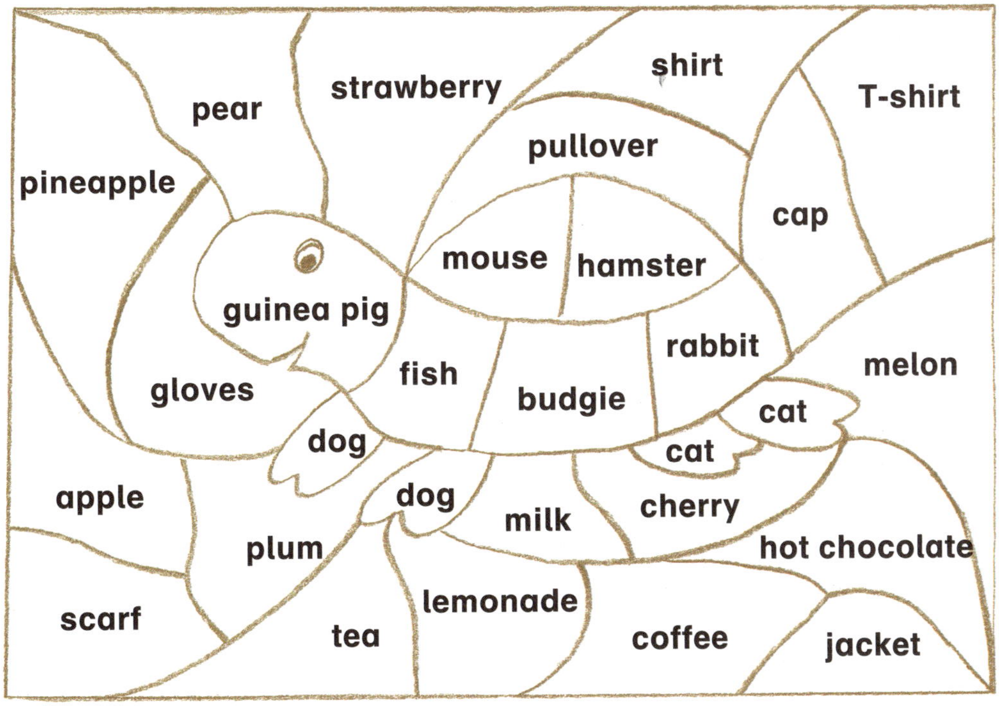

I can see a ______________________ .

3. Guess the pets. Write.

____

4. Trace the lines and write.

A ______________ likes  .

A ______________ likes  .

A ______________________________  .

______________________________  .

______________________________  .

mouse
cat
guinea pig
dog
rabbit

1. Write and draw lines.

Schreibe zuerst unter jedes Bild die passende Jahreszeit. Ordne dann den Jahreszeiten die Monate zu.

spring **summer**
autumn **winter**

June

May

August

April

July

March

It's ______________ . It's ______________ .

September

January

November

October

February

December

It's ______________ . It's ______________ .

2. Write the 12 months in the correct order.

1. ______________ 2. ______________ 3. ______________

4. ______________ 5. ______________ 6. ______________

7. ______________ 8. ______________ 9. ______________

10. ______________ 11. ______________ 12. ______________

3. Read and tick the correct answer.

Easter is in ...

◯ winter ◯ summer ◯ spring.

Christmas is in ...

◯ December ◯ November ◯ September.

Halloween is in ...

◯ April ◯ October ◯ February.

The summer holidays are in ...

◯ January ◯ March ◯ July/August.

4. What can you see? Write.

pond
butter-fly
tree
grass
frog
flower

I can see a ____________ .

I can see a ____________ .

I can see a ____________ .

I can see a ____________ .

I can see ____________ .

I can see a ____________ .

5. Find the months. Draw lines and write.

Octo-
Novem-
Jul-
Janua-
Mar-
-ber
Decem-
Septem-

6. What can you see?
Colour the spring words green, the summer words yellow, the autumn words brown and the winter words blue.

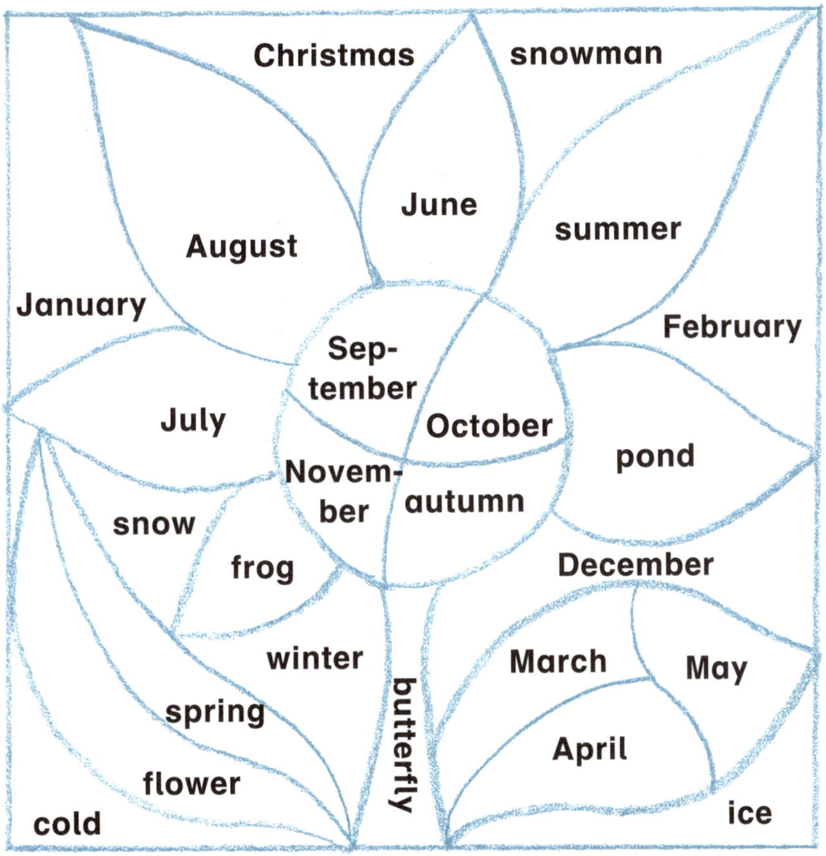

I can see a .

1. These animals live on a farm. Write the words and draw lines.

h _ rs _

c _ w

sh _ _ p

d _ ck

g _ _ s _

p _ g

h _ n

horse pig hen sheep goose cow duck

2. What do they say? Write.

A duck says quak-quak.

A ________ says cluck-cluck.

A ________ says oink-oink.

A ________ says neigh-neigh.

A ________ says honk-honk.

A ________ says baa-baa.

A ________ says moo-moo.

duck goose horse pig hen sheep cow

3. Read the comic.

On the farm

1. Colour the British flag – The Union Jack.

2. What can you see in the pictures? Write.

Buckingham Palace **Tower Bridge** **London Eye** **Big Ben**

3. Read the comic.

Sally in London

morning
afternoon
evening
night

blue
yellow
green
red
black
grey
purple
brown
white
orange
pink

one two three four five six seven
eight nine ten

lollipop lady picture poster

computer board

chalk

pencil case

teacher

pupil

desk

pencil

book

ruler

rubber

folder pen schoolbag glue scissors

arms	ears	hands	legs	fingers	toes
nose	eyes	tooth/teeth	foot/feet	knees	

racing car   doll   computer game   castle   spaceship
ball   helicopter   lorry   inline skates   teddy bear

jacket

skirt

shirt

T-shirt

shoes

socks

boots

cap

dress

pullover

woolly hat

scarf

gloves

anorak

a pair of trousers

a pair of shorts

It's _ _ _ _ _ .

It's _ _ _ _ _ .

It's _ _ _ _ _ .

It's _ _ _ _ _ _ .

It's _ _ _ _ _ and _ _ _ .

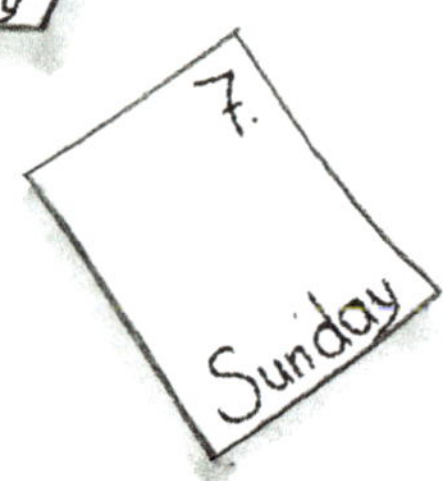

It's _ _ _ _ _ and _ _ _ _ .

sunny **rainy** **snowy**
cloudy **foggy** **windy**
cold **hot**

grandmother/grandma   aunt   father   uncle   sister
mother   dad   brother   mum   grandfather/ grandpa

hot chocolate coffee
tea milk coke
orange juice lemonade
water apple juice

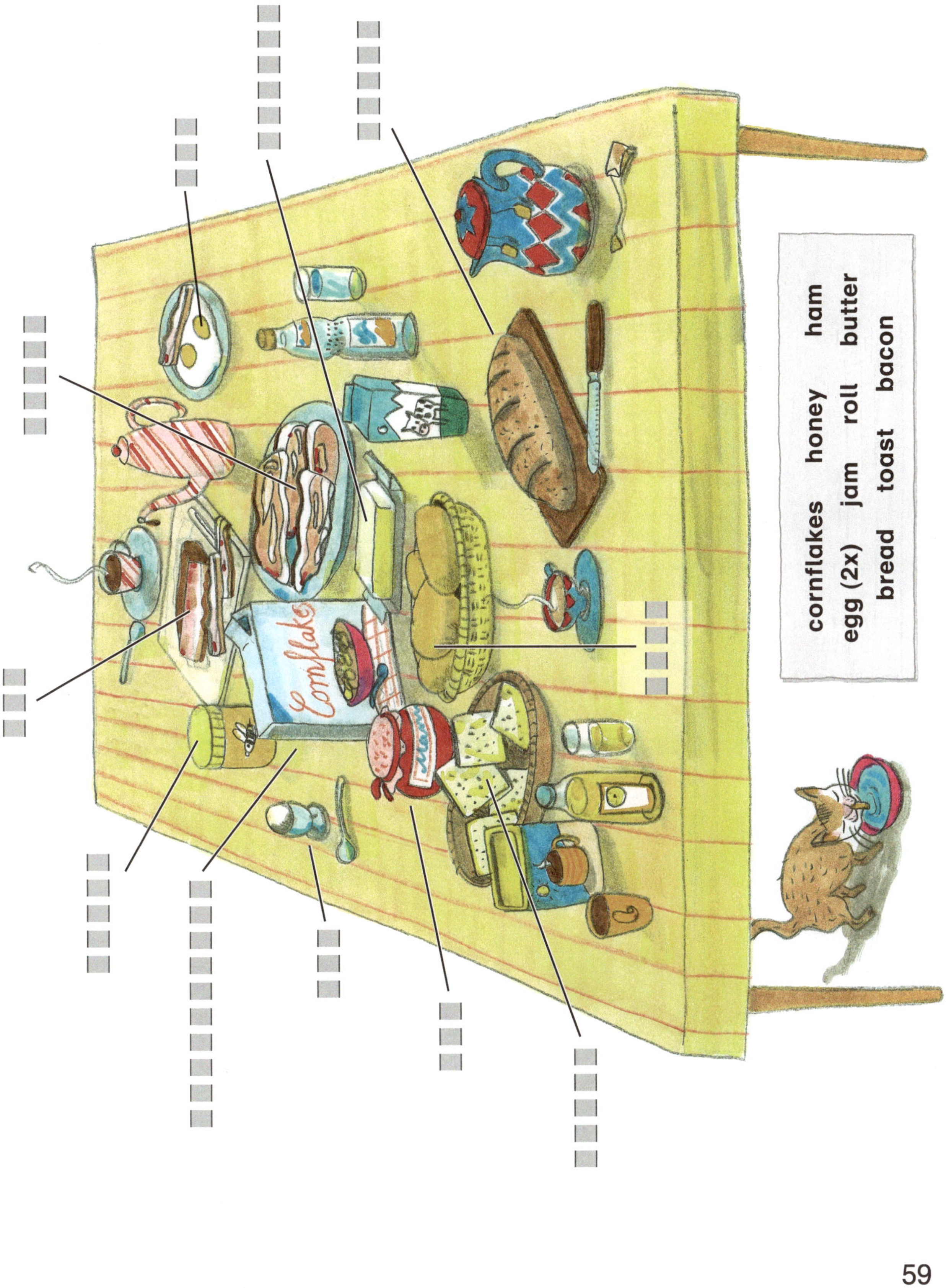
cornflakes honey ham
egg (2x) jam roll butter
bread toast bacon
Cornflakes

melon lemon banana
plum cherry orange
strawberry pear
apple pineapple

budgie **tortoise** **hamster** **cat** **guinea pig** **dog**
rabbit **mouse** **fish**

grass

Easter egg

sun

butterfly

tree

flower

frog

pond

March
April
May

June
July
August

It's spring.

It's summer.

snowman

pumpkin

September
October
November

December
January
February

It's autumn.

It's winter.

hen	**pig**	**horse**	**cow**	**goose**	**sheep**	**duck**

Buckingham Palace
Tower Bridge
London Eye
Big Ben
Union Jack
the Queen